CW01024102

Let's Start a Scrapbook for Boys

Written by Lisa Regan
Scrapbook layouts designed by Sigrid Schroeder
Layout by custardfish

TOP THAT! Kids™
Published by Top That! Publishing plc
Tide Mill Way, Woodbridge, Suffolk, IP12 1AP, UK
www.topthatpublishing.com
Top That! Kids is a Trademark of Top That! Publishing plc
Copyright © 2006 Top That! Publishing plc
All rights reserved
0 2 4 6 8 9 7 5 3 1
Printed and bound in China

Contents

Scrapbooking Techniques

Scrapbooking Projects

Let's Start Scrapbooking

What exactly IS scrapbooking? It's a way of storing all your memories for other people to see, using photographs and other items stuck into your scrapbook. It's a bit like putting your photos in an album, but looks even better because of all the extra things you can put on the page.

Telling your Stories

It's a great hobby, and you don't need to be very 'arty' to give it a go. The basic skills are easy – cutting and sticking. With a bit of practice, you can soon make pages that look great, and tell the story of your life. There's no 'right' or 'wrong' way to do it – you can do whatever looks good to you. This book outlines the basic techniques used in scrapbooking to help you make your pages look different from each other and not just like a photo album. There are also some projects later in the book to give you ideas on how to make your pages.

Gathering your Ideas

Before you get started, there are some things you should do. First, flick through the pages of this book to see what kinds of designs you can try. Then sort through all of your photos and decide which people and events you want in your scrapbook. Finally, gather together any extra items you want to include as mementoes or just as decorations - these are often called embellishments (see page 34).

Buying a Scrapbook

Scrapbooking albums can be bought from craft shops in a massive range of shapes and sizes. The projects in this book have all been produced on squares measuring 210 mm x 210 mm, but buy whichever size best fits your layout. Scrapbooks don't have to be expensive – there are plenty of traditional scrapbooks out there filled with sugar paper sheets that will work well. However, if you want to keep your scrapbook for many years, it is worth buying a scrapbook with 'acid free' pages since some papers deteriorate over time.

Layouts

The layout of a page is the way that you position all of your items to show them off properly. The best way to create a finished page that you're happy with is to experiment with different arrangements, or layouts, using a selection of photos and embellishments. Don't stick anything down until you're really sure where everything needs to be.

Choose a Theme

Scrapbookers usually choose a different theme for each page of their scrapbook. You could dedicate a page to the day you went surfing, or make several pages for an adventure holiday. Look through photos of your favourite events and choose the best ones. Put them with other mementoes, like tickets and maps.

How many Photos?

There's no set number of photos you need for one page. You might want several small photos of the same size, or a big one as a focus point with a couple of smaller ones. Look closely at what's in the photos to see if you can make them smaller (crop) – see page 18.

Focus Points

Scrapbookers often divide their page into nine sections, like a noughts and crosses grid. The four points where the lines cross near the middle of the page are the main focus points for your most important items. The grid also splits the page into thirds (either across or down) if you want to feature three items equally.

> **Tip**
>
> Look through books and magazines to see how other people design pages. See how different styles are achieved through different layouts.

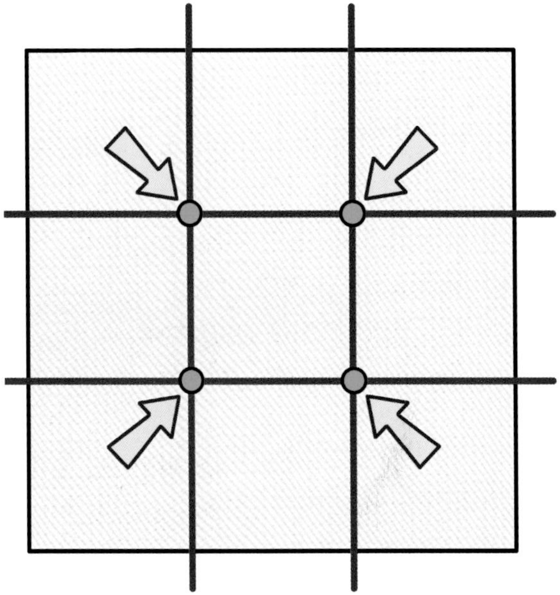

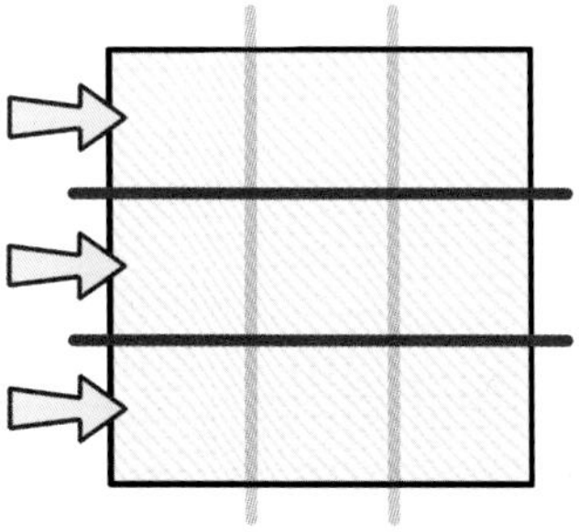

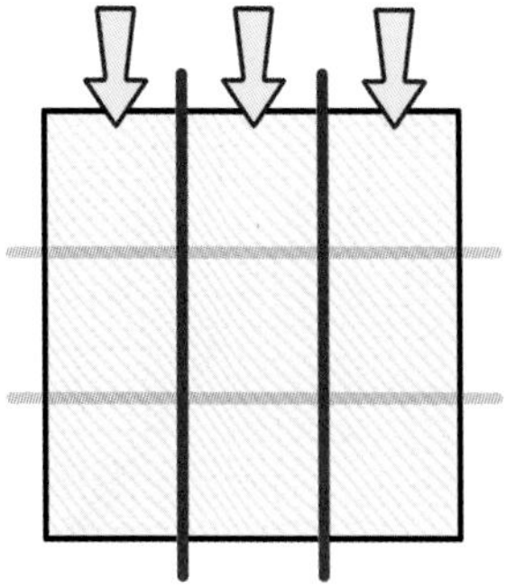

Give it Space

Two of the main ways to make your page look smarter are by framing your photos (see page 29) or matting (see page 14). These techniques draw attention to the focus points of your page. Allow space around your items when you're planning your layout.

Shapes and Colour

The shapes you choose for your photos, and the colours you use on the whole page, should be gleaned from the photos themselves. Study the photos to see what shapes work best. Let the photos help you decide on an overall colour scheme.

Basic Templates

The shapes on your page are important for the overall look. Experiment with fun shapes like stars, diamonds and even balloons. Follow the instructions here to cut your photo into a simple oval.

Draw an oval template on scrap paper. Cut it out and place it over the photo, like a frame. When you're sure that it's the right shape and size to fit the photo, draw around the shape using a soft pencil. Cut out the oval carefully with sharp scissors and rub out any pencil that is left.

Don't fill your page with too many crazy shapes. The usual shapes for photographs are rectangles, squares, circles and ovals.

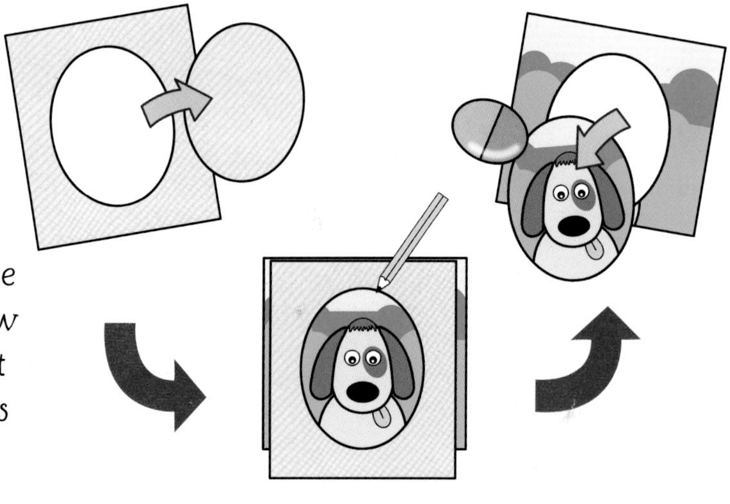

Colours and Themes

Choose colours that work well with the theme of your page. Here, the photos of the beach with their blue, green and yellow tones work well with the papers shown to the right. Camouflage colours such as brown, green and beige work well with photos of outdoor events.

Tip

Choose two striking colours from your picture and use them in blocks as the background to the page. This technique is called colour blocking.

Bringing it Out

Study the colours of the photo to see what colours you could use in the background. For example, if your photo is of a bright red dream car, use the same bright red in your matting (see page 14), as shown in this picture to the left.

Backgrounds

The colours in your background, and the extra items you use for decoration, are as important as the photos themselves. Your background should draw attention to the main parts of your page, but not overpower them.

Textures, Colours and Patterns

Experiment with backgrounds made up of different coloured, patterned and textured papers. Buy your papers in craft shops or use what you can find! Newspapers and wrapping paper both make lively backgrounds. If buying from a craft shop, take your photos with you so that you can match your theme exactly.

Tip

Use stamps to make your own personalised patterned backgrounds - see page 24.

Lead the Eye

When you're designing your backgrounds, use lines and shapes to lead the eye to the main photographs. Stripes and borders can be used on the pages to point to the focus points. For a really fancy background, be inspired by details from the photographs. For example, use camouflage netting, dog tags and footprints for an outward bound or extreme sports page.

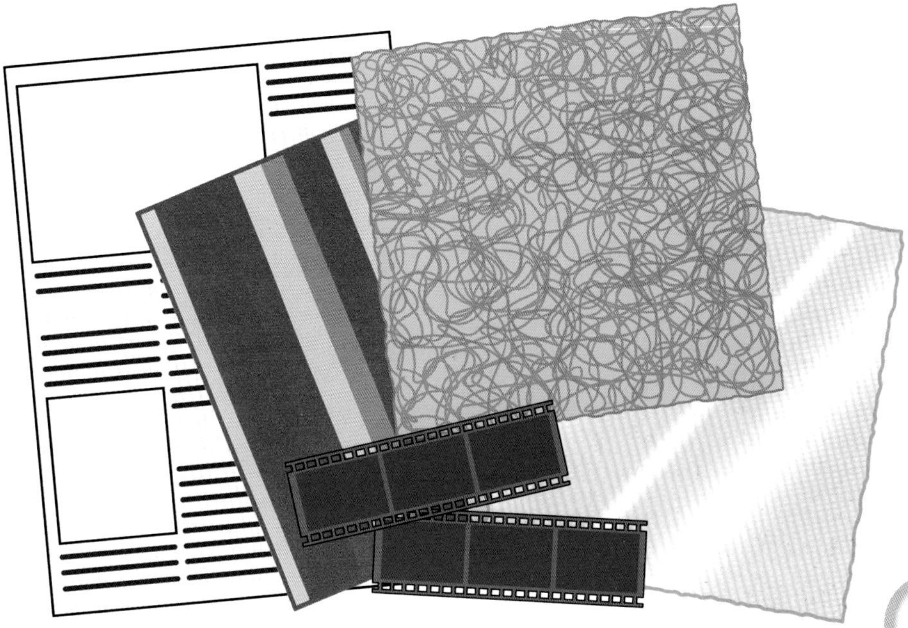

Touch 'n' Feel

Think carefully about textures. It's great to run your fingers over a scrapbook page and feel rough sandpaper, smooth foil or bumpy corrugated card.

Funky Background Ideas

Collect together as many things as you can to use in your backgrounds. Wrapping paper, foil, fabric, tissue paper, wallpaper and even old Christmas cards will all give different effects. Old negatives from 35 mm cameras make a great background – cut your pictures to stick on top of the unwanted photos in the negatives. Photocopy items that are more bulky and use the copies as backgrounds.

Paper

Paper is your most important resource! Scrunched or smooth, rolled or torn – there's loads you can do to give an extra dimension to each project.

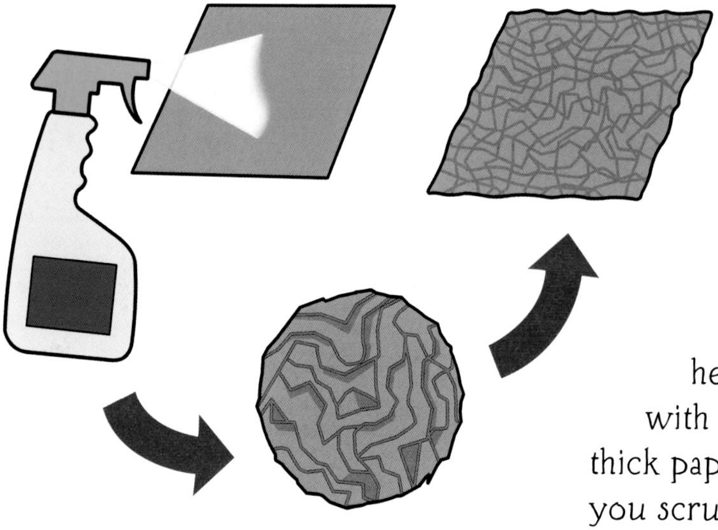

Scrunch and Smooth

For a textured effect, screw up your paper into a ball and then open it out and smooth it with your hand. You could even 'set' the creases with an iron on a low heat (you MUST ask for adult help with this). If you're using very thick paper, spray it with water before you scrunch it. Let it dry completely before sticking it in place.

No Scissors Required

Instead of cutting the paper with scissors, tear it to get a rough, scruffy edge. Try tearing different types of paper, then looking at the edges. Sometimes it tears in a nice straight line. Sometimes it goes completely bonkers! Certain coloured papers tear to reveal a white edge, which can be used to great effect.

Tip

Use creased blue paper for watery pics like a trip to the aquarium or a diving adventure.

Roll With It

After you've torn the paper, make tiny scissor snips into the edge. Place on a flat surface, and roll the edge with your fingers. Frame a photo and roll the edges for a wild look!

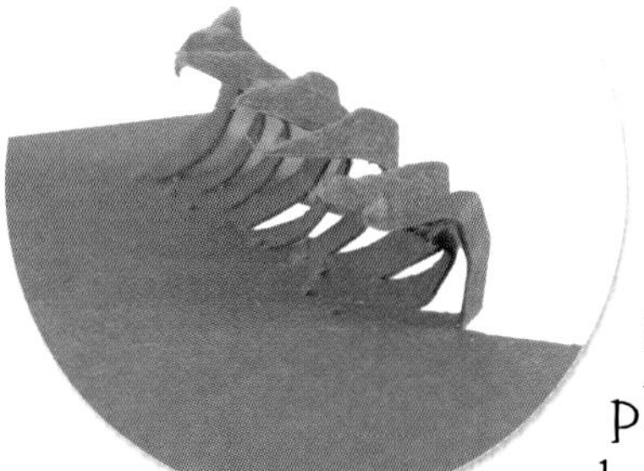

Jagged and Fluffy

If you're using thick card, you can add another cool effect to your photos. Hold your piece of card parallel with the floor. Scrape the edge of the card with the blade of a pair of sharp scissors, working away from your body for safety. Carry on until the edge is jagged, or even longer until it becomes fluffy. This effect can be used to give an old-fashioned feel if it's used on faded colours with old photos, or it can look really cool if it's used with bright colours and modern designs.

Matting

Matting is one of the main techniques used in scrapbooking. Basically, it's layering pieces of paper or card behind the photos to give them a border.

Keep it Simple

You can use a single mat behind a photo, or several layers of matting. Don't get carried away and use lots of layers behind every photo on your page. Keep it simple for the best effect. To mat a photo with a straight edge, glue the photo in place in the corner of your matting paper with a small amount of paper showing around the outside edges. Measure the same amount around the other edges and trim it to fit.

Triple Strength

For an important photo, use three different layers of matting. The second layer can be a patterned paper, or have a decorative edge made by tearing it or cutting it with fancy scissors.

Guides and Templates

If you have cropped a photo into a square or a circle (see page 18), you'll need a template for your mat. For these basic shapes, simply draw around a household object, such as a CD case or an upturned mug or glass. For more complex shapes – a footprint or a big splat, for example – it's worth buying a specialist disc set, which will guide your pencil around the edge of the shape, making a perfect, larger copy.

Tip

You can tear the edges of your matting as on page 13 to make it more interesting.

Colour and Constrast

Choose your matting paper carefully to complement the colours of your photograph and background. Sometimes, a simple cream mat is most effective to make a photo – such as the dog (above) – stand out. Then choose bright colours to constrast with the pale cream, like the red and purple matted background here.

Journalling

This is a term used in scrapbooking and simply means any writing you put on your pages. This can be headings and titles, labels, quotes and thoughts or even lines from songs.

Summing it Up

Sometimes journalling is as straightforward as writing alongside each photo to say what it is. You can use a single block of writing to describe the whole of the page, as if you were telling somebody what it's all about.

Styles and Colours

If you like, you can decorate your page with funky writing. Choose words that sum up the theme of the page and write them in different styles and colours, like the examples shown in the box above.

LOVE TRUST
FAITHFUL
DIRTY
LICKY SMELLY

If you're not very good with words, choose your favourite line from a song or book, or look up quotations on the internet.

Stencil, Sticker, Transfer?

There are many different ways you can write your text. If you have neat handwriting, write labels and stick them on to your background. If you prefer, use stencils, stickers or transfers. Ask someone who is good at calligraphy to write out words for you to trace, copy or cut out. There are some great pens in the shops (look for waterproof, fade-resistant, acid-free pens) with fancy nibs to give special effects to your writing.

Tip

For a sparkly heading, mark out your words with a glue stick then shake glitter on top.

Help me, Computer!

If you're not fond of your own handwriting style, use your computer to find a font that you like. Type your text and print it onto your chosen paper in a very pale grey. Write over the top of the printout in pen and neatly cut out your journalling.

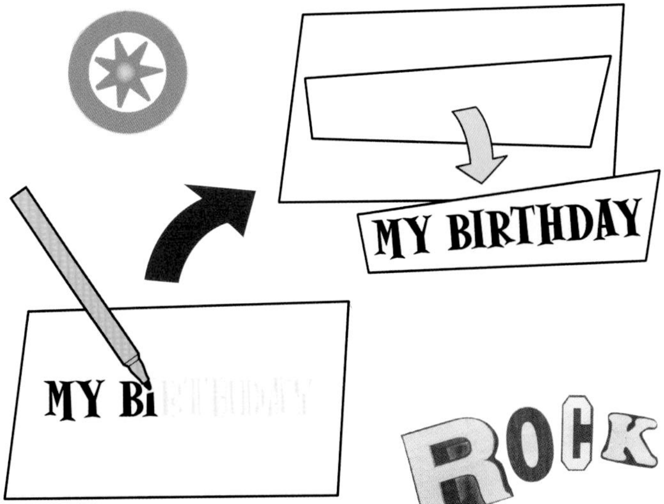

On a Roll

Cut out letters and words from newspapers and magazines to create stylish journalling. Stick them on a curve for a cool finish.

Cropping Photos

You'll need to learn the best ways to cut and shape your photos if you want to design cool pages. If you don't trim some of them, you won't fit many on a page, and your pages will look more like an ordinary photo album than a scrapbook. However, don't go mad and chop up all your best pictures!

Choosing the Subject

Lay out all of your chosen photos before you start cropping. Some photos, like the landscape of the sea (top right) look best left as they are, but with rounded corners for a neat finish. Other photos may have lots of dull items in the background, so it's best to cut a circle with the focal point in the centre, such as the dog photo (right). Some contain a tiny item of interest – like the rabbit (far right) – so cut it out of the photo completely.

Location, Location!

When you're cropping, don't try to do too much on a page. Be careful not to crop away background items that are important. There's little point having a page of holiday photos from Egypt if you can't see the Pyramids behind you in the background!

Neat Squares

Learning to crop neat squares takes a bit of practice. Choose your focal point, then measure an equal distance up, down, left and right of this point, and mark each with a dot. Join the dots with a ruler and mark with a soft pencil. Check your lines are straight before cutting.

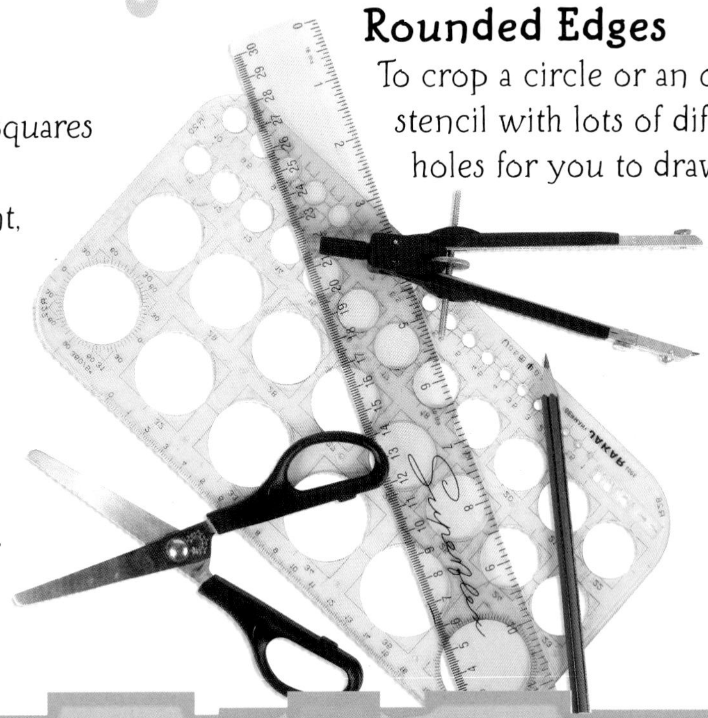

Rounded Edges

To crop a circle or an oval, use a stencil with lots of different-sized holes for you to draw around, or use a pair of compasses. For rounded edges, draw around a coin in each corner and cut around the line.

Get Stuck In!

There are different ways you can attach items to your page. Choose your adhesive carefully according to the item you want to stick in your scrapbook. Wherever possible, use glue that is labelled 'acid-free' to keep your scrapbook in good condition over the years.

Choosing your Glue

Photos and paper can be stuck in place with paper glue. Make sure the glue goes all the way to the edge of the item you are sticking, so that it doesn't curl up. If you are gluing fabric or very thin paper, the glue will show through. Use double-sided tape or sticky tabs (bought from craft shops) instead. Spray mount (spray-on glue from a tin) is useful for sticking delicate items, but always use it in a well-ventilated area since the fumes are dangerous and unpleasant. Craft glue is ideal for sticking heavier paper items.

Heavy Items

Some embellishments (see page 34) may be heavy or bulky, and therefore harder to stick in place. Glue dots should be strong enough to hold items such as keys, badges and metal items.

Stitching it Together

Sewing can also be used to hold things in place and decorate your scrapbook at the same time. If necessary, use a small amount of glue first to keep the item completely secure before you sew. To sew heavy card, use a needle and a ruler to make the holes before you sew. Carefully press the needle along your card at regular intervals (using a ruler to keep things straight). It will be much easier to pass the needle and thread through once you've punched these holes.

Using Vellum

Vellum is see-through paper, a bit like tracing paper, but thicker. It's available in different colours and with patterns printed onto it. Find it in craft shops.

Toning it Down

Vellum tones down the colour of anything underneath, so you can use it to add a subtle effect to bright backgrounds. It can be torn and stuck in layers to add texture, as at the bottom of the project shown right.

Using as Matting

Try using vellum when you're matting photographs. It helps to draw attention to a good picture without adding lots of bright colour. Be careful how you attach it, though – since vellum is see-through, your glue will show unless it is hidden beneath the photo itself.

Added Extras

Vellum is great for using when you're journalling. Use it like tracing paper to copy fancy writing with a permanent pen. Cut the vellum to the size and shape you want, and attach it to your page with glue or by hanging it on thread through a punched hole. You can use it in the same way to copy pictures or logos, like a school badge or a skate logo.

Tip

Vellum looks great attached with novel items such as brads (split pins) or stitching. See pages 34 and 35 for more about this.

Handy Holder

Vellum pockets can be used to hold items that you want to be visible, but don't want to glue down. To make one, copy the outline shown onto your sheet. Cut it out, and fold along the dotted lines. Stick the sides down, then stick the back of the pocket to your page.

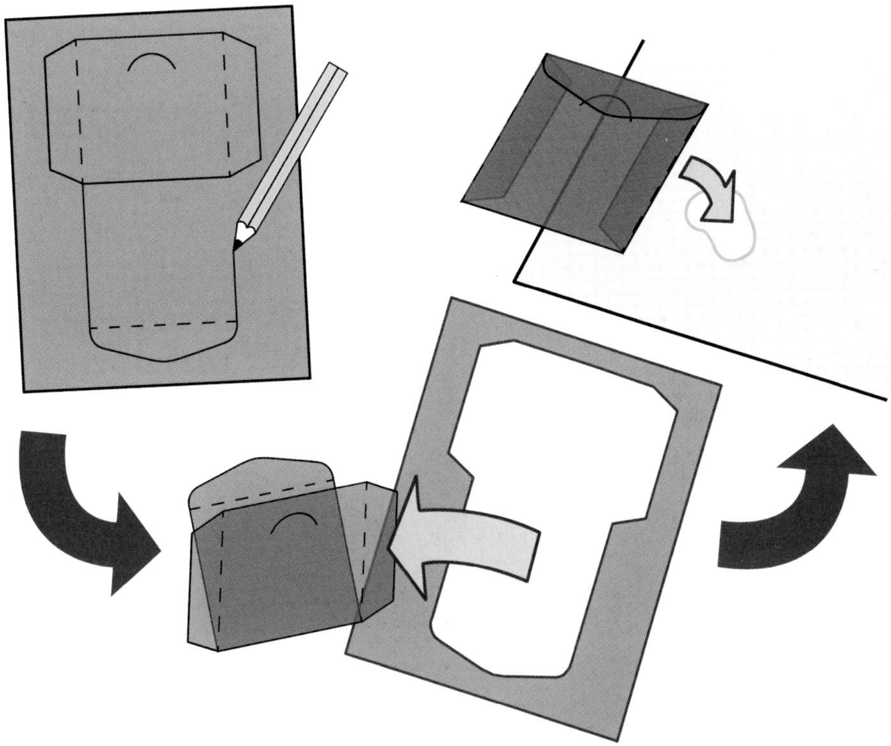

Stamping

Stamping is a great way to add decorations to your page. You can repeat a pattern in the background on a single page, or across several pages of your scrapbook.

Stamping Step-by-Step

First, get hold of some rubber stamps. If they come with an ink pad, great, but you might want to mix paint to your chosen colour. Roll the stamper across your ink pad, or dab it in your paint, then gently press and release the stamper onto your page. Let the paint dry before you cut the paper and stick it in place. Only stamp straight onto the page if you're confident!

Tip

Remember, whatever your design looks like on the stamp, it will print in reverse (like a mirror image) when you press it onto paper!

Sponge Stamp

You can buy rubber stamps from craft shops, but you can easily make your own. To make a sponge stamp, you'll need one sponge block and another sponge cut into layers. Draw your design onto one of the sponge layers, cut it out and stick it onto the block. Simple shapes, like the star and splat shown here work well.

Potato Stamping

For something more temporary, you can make a potato stamp. Ask an adult to cut a potato in half. Then sketch your shape out in felt-tip pen, and ask an adult to help you cut away the area around it, leaving a raised shape about 1 cm deep. Blot the starchy potato juice onto kitchen paper before attempting to print with the stamp. Try printing a border of brightly coloured stars onto a page featuring your kid brother, or a footprint pattern across an animal page.

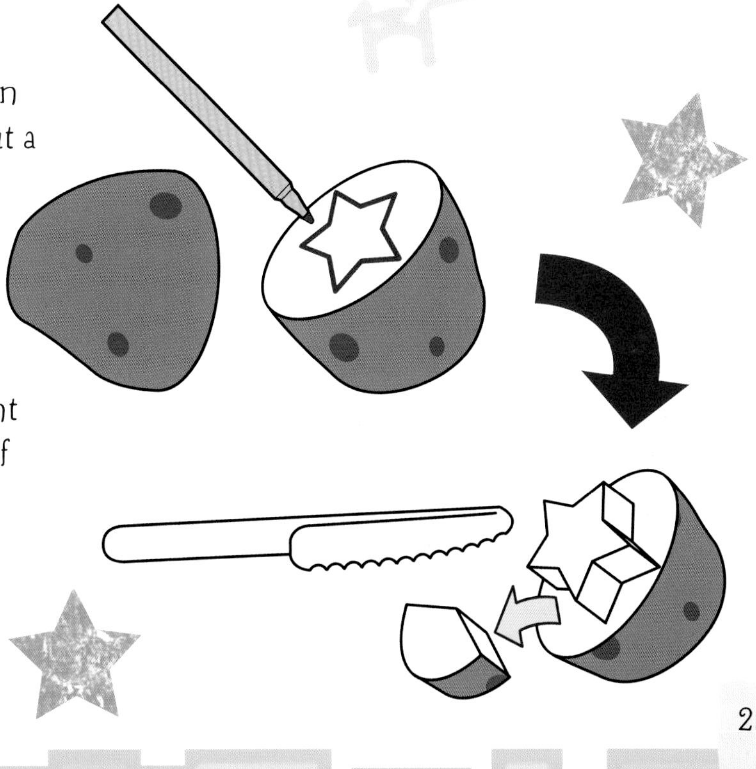

Stickers and Punches

An easy way to brighten up your scrapbook pages is with stickers or cut-out items. They can be used as borders or scattered around the whole page.

Punching Effects

Shop-bought punches make small, neat motifs in any paper or card you choose. Punch out several to decorate your page and stick down randomly for a scattered look. Try overlapping punched shapes of different colours to add contrast and depth.

Adding Dimension

Punched shapes can be made to look 3-D by raising them off the page slightly using sticky tabs (see page 20). Peel the tab away from its protective backing, and fix your shape to the sticky side that's exposed. Then trim around the shape exactly, before removing the backing from the other side of the tab. Stick the shape to your page.

Sticky Letters

You can buy packs of alphabet stickers, and use them to spell out titles, names and dates of special occasions. Spell out your message on top of the sticker paper first of all, with at least half of the letters sticking off the paper. Make sure the spacing is even, and then position the message onto your scrapbook page. Now you can press down the top half of the letters, slide away the sticker paper, and smooth the bottom half into place.

Tip

To avoid making spelling mistakes when positioning stickers, write down your journalling first on a scrap piece of paper. Then you don't have to concentrate too much!

What to Buy?

There's a huge choice of stickers out there. Look for packs of themed stickers (such as sports), or choose a book of stickers with your name on. Keep your eyes out for stickers with the 'wow' factor, too, such as holograms and those with luminous or shiny finishes.

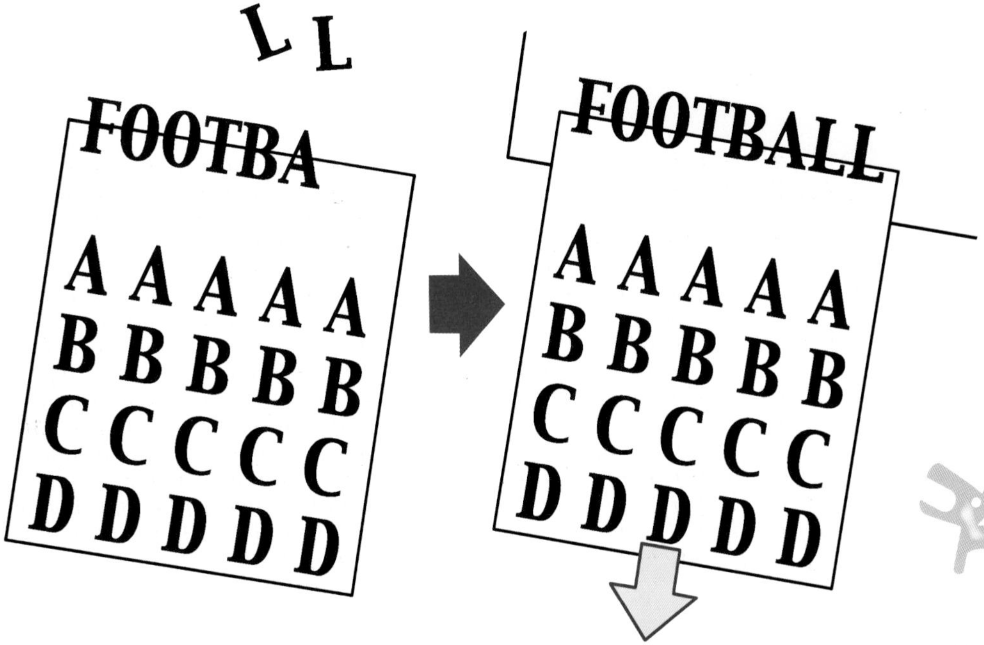

Customizing Cut-outs

Shaped card pieces will really liven up your pages. They can be bought as die-cuts, which means they're punched into a card sheet so that you can push them out – or you can make your own.

Making Card Letters

Card letters are very useful for headings and titles. Use a stencil to draw your own letters and then cut them out with sharp scissors. You can draw around these letters to make several sets of letters. Try making two sets of letters to spell a word, like SUPERCARS. Stick them so that the second set of letters is underneath the first, with only a fraction showing like a shadow. You can make the shadow set sit slightly above or below, and to the left or the right.

Customizing your Cut-outs

Add some bling to your pages with glittery versions of images found in catalogues and magazines. Cut out the shapes you want, then mount them onto card. Add glue to the areas you want to highlight, then shake glitter over the top. Wait until the glue is dry before shaking off the excess glitter.

Tip

After you have cut out your shapes, use the hole that is left as a template to apply chalks through (see page 30).

Make a Cardboard Frame

Cardboard frames are easy to make. Draw your frame onto card and cut around the outside edge. Then cut out the middle bit. Place your frame over your photo, and wiggle it around until you're happy with the bit of the photo that peeps through. Hold the frame and photo together, then draw around the inner section with a soft pencil. Cut around the pencil mark, leaving a small border. Glue around this border, and stick your photo to the frame.

Using Chalk

Chalk is a versatile tool that can be used in lots of ways. It warms up pale paper, adds colour and softness and can also give an aged look to your papers and photos. Scrapbooking chalk is the easiest type to use, but you can still achieve great effects with the alternative type.

Adding Definition

Define the edges of your photos using chalk rubbed on cotton wool for a soft effect, or apply using a cotton bud for sharp edges.

Tip

If you make a mistake with the chalk, you can quickly rub it out with a special putty eraser like those used by artists.

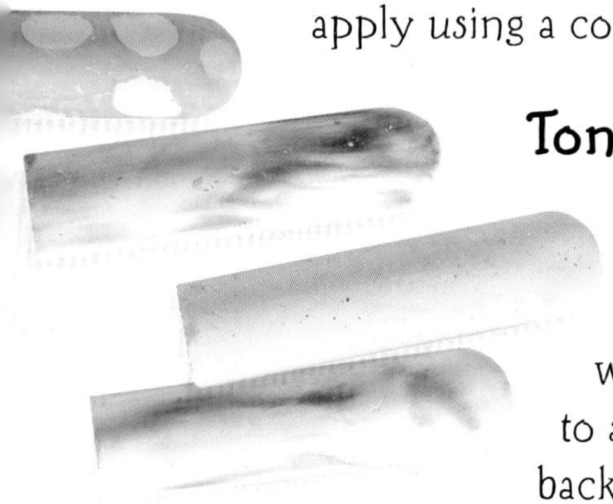

Toning it Down

Make white paper look less startling and harsh by applying a small amount of pale-coloured chalk. Rub it on in circles with a piece of cotton wool. Always start with a little chalk, and build it up gradually to avoid mistakes. Hold the paper next to your photo and background to make sure you achieve the subtle effect you want.

Adding on the Years

To make a photo look aged, try rubbing the edges with sandpaper, and then applying chalk to the sanded areas. You can use two similar colours to give a misty effect, as in the rabbit photo (top right), where purple chalk has been layered over the blue.

Star Chalk Effects

You can achieve two very cool looks with a cardboard cut-out. For a shape with a soft centre and neat edges (bottom left), make a cardboard frame and keep the middle part. Press the frame firmly onto your chosen paper and dab chalk onto the hole with cotton wool. For a neat shape with softly fading edges (bottom right), place the middle part of your frame onto your page, and chalk around the edges before lifting it away.

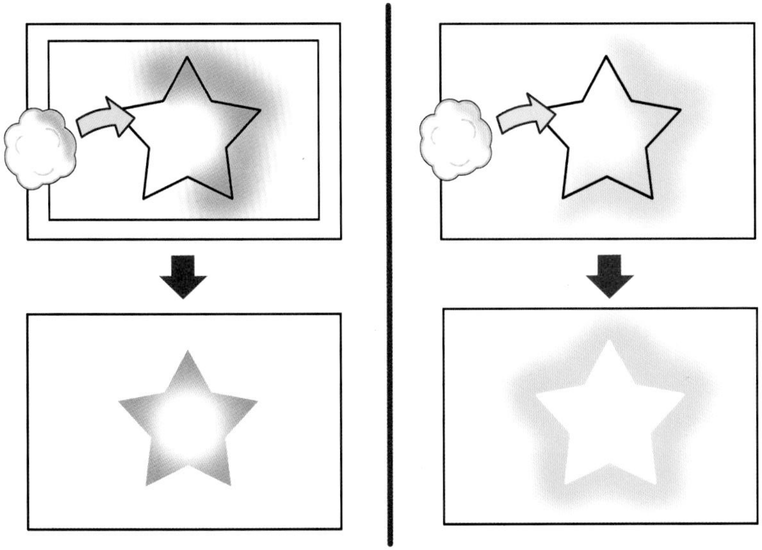

A Word about Layers

Layering different colours of chalk takes practice, so experiment on scrap paper first. Start with the lightest colours and add small amounts of the darker colours afterwards,

Memorabilia

If a scrapbook is meant to tell a story, there are lots of items that you can include in its pages! Memorabilia is the general name for all these items, such as tickets from a football match, badges and party decorations.

A Day to Remember

Make a page for a special trip, such as a day at the beach, a visit to a museum or a football or rugby match. Keep all the little things that you pick up during the day – your bus and train tickets might not seem interesting now, but they'll remind you of exactly where you went, and when, after the memories have faded.

Tip

Whenever you're out and about, always think about things that you could collect for your scrapbook. The day you score your first goal, for example, take a team photo, and save a bit of mud from your football boots!

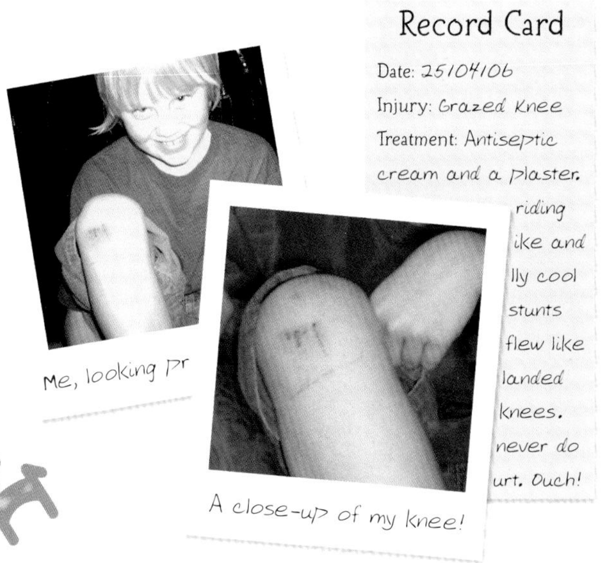

Telling Tales

Remember how proud you were of that giant purple bruise you got scoring that winning goal? Then why not create a page dedicated to your injuries? You could take pictures of your cuts and bruises, then create a table to record them in, as shown here. Write down the date it happened, how you treated the injury, and tell a funny story about how it happened.

While You're Away

Holidays provide lots of memorabilia for your scrapbooking. Alongside holiday photos, include postcards, details of where you stayed, foreign coins and scraps of newspapers from the area.

The Natural Look

If you've collected some nice leaves while playing outside, then you can dry them out before sticking them to your page. Place the leaves between two sheets of paper, then put the paper between the pages of a heavy book. Check in a few weeks' time, and they should be ready.

Embellishments

Many of the sample scrapbook pages you have seen include small items of decoration to finish the look of a page. Some of them have been mentioned already, but here's a quick run down of things you can use for your projects.

Holding it Together

Split pins (often called brads by scrapbookers) can be used to decorate the page, or to hold other items in place. To attach a photo to a piece of card, hold the photo firmly in position on top of the card. Make holes in the corners of the photo with a hole punch. Push the closed brads through the holes. Separate and flatten the metal prongs on the reverse of the card, as shown, to hold the photo securely.

Wibble, Wobble!

Stick goggle eyes to the people in your photos to make your pictures look funny – plus, they really draw attention to your project!

Get Knotting

String or ribbon can be glued on the page in lines, or tied in knots and bows. Try wrapping it around and around a frame before you stick the frame down. Or use a hole punch to make two neat holes in a frame, and thread string out through the holes to tie at the front. Use it to attach tags or other labels.

Metal and Wire

Buy metal inserts or use jewellery wire to add a cool, metallic look. Jewellery wire can be twisted into shapes and letters to decorate the pages. Metal items like small keys, nuts and washers look great stuck on a page as a frame or just as decoration.

Birthday Boy

Cake decorations and badges from birthday cards are quite bulky, but should stay stuck to your page with glue dots.

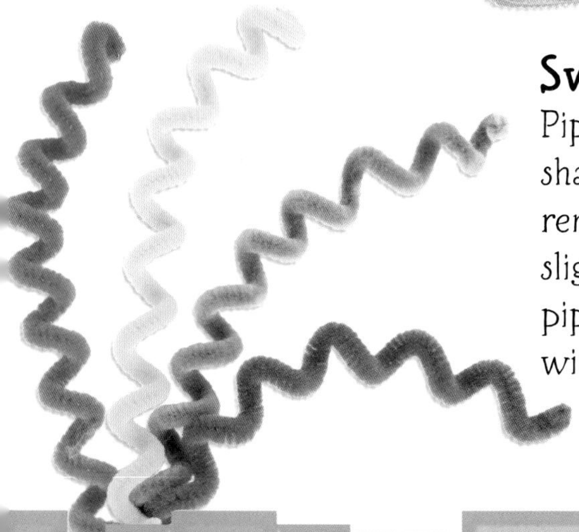

Swizzle Sticks

Pipe cleaners make great bendy shapes. Wrap one around a pencil, remove the pencil, then squash slightly before sticking the pipe cleaner to your page with strong glue.

Special People

You could design a page for each member of your family. This one is for a brilliant dad, but the techniques described can be adapted for anyone!

You will need:

- two photos of your dad (you can be in them too!)
- a black felt-tip pen • glue
- a pencil • a ruler • scissors

Papers:

- light green paper • dark green tissue paper
- coloured scraps • white paper • red card

Embellishments:

- washers and nuts • a picture of a TV set
- a reminder of dad's favourite sport

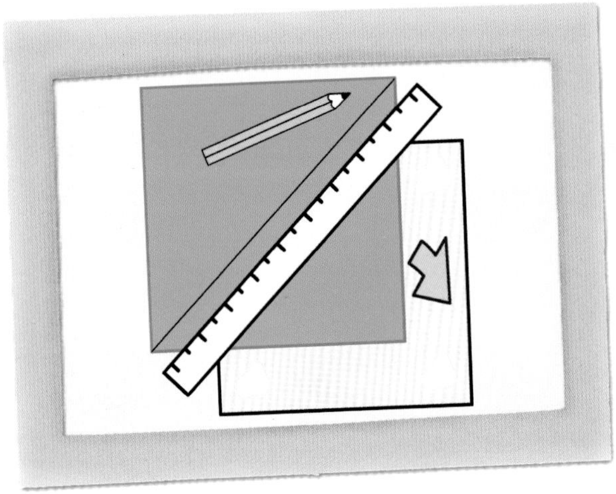

1 To make the background, cut your light green paper to the exact size of your scrapbook page. Divide it from corner to corner with a pencil and ruler. Stick the paper onto your scrapbook page.

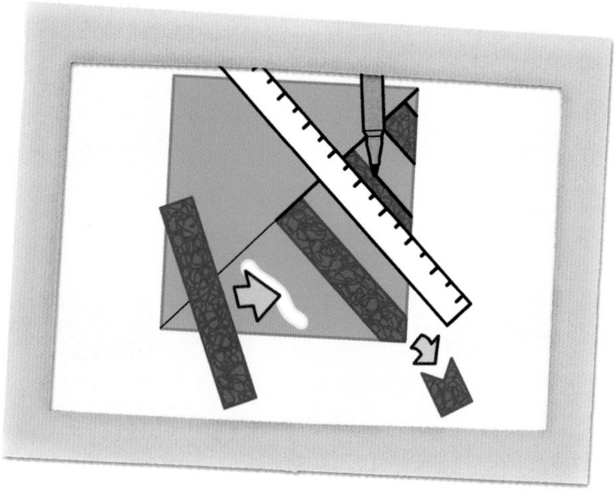

2 Cut equal strips of dark green tissue paper and stick them from the diagonal line to the edge of the page. Trim the strips to keep the page edge neat. Using a ruler to help keep a steady hand, highlight the strips with black lines drawn with your felt-tip pen.

3 Frame the picture of your dad with the red card. (See page 29 for instructions on framing photos). Stick the nuts and washers around the edge of the frame to give the impression that he spends a lot of time in the garage!

4 Stick your framed photo in place on your scrapbook page. Use glue dots or sticky tabs if the nuts and washers have made it heavy.

5 To make a medal, cut out a piece of card to the grey shape shown on the right. Then stick your coloured scraps of paper onto the top part to make colourful stripes. Outline the circle and the stripes in black pen, then write on 'NO. 1 DAD'. Add white paper matting, and stick the medal onto your page.

Scrapattack Tip:
If you can print the words on a computer, they'll look much neater and more official for your medal.

6 Carefully cut around your TV picture, then cut a hole in the middle to remove the 'screen'. Use your TV to frame the photo of your dad (see page 29), then glue it in place on your page.

7 What's your dad's favourite sport? Try to find an item that shows the sport he likes best, like this mini plastic dartboard. Glue it onto coloured paper and add the words 'FAVE SPORT' with a felt-tip pen. Cut around the shape and add white matting before fixing it in place on the page.

8 Finally, think of a few words about what your dad is like. Funny, kind, clever? Write them onto scraps of coloured paper and mat them with white paper. Add this journalling to fill any spaces on your page.

Scrapattack Tip:
Use a mixture of hand-written and computer-printed journalling on your page for a neat, but informal, effect.

FAVE
SPORT
HAPPY
FUNNY
CLEVER
KIND
FAVE HOBBY
No.1
DAD

Animal Crackers

Keep a record of great days out by adding them to pages in your scrapbook. Everyone loves a trip to the animal park – as long as they're not kept behind with the monkeys by mistake!

You will need:
• animal photos • glue • black paint • a footprint stamp (see page 24) • coloured pencils • a black felt-tip pen • pressed leaves (see page 33) • scissors

Papers:
• yellow paper • red paper • brown paper • blue paper • white paper

Embellishments:
• an entrance ticket

1 Use your yellow paper for the background. Cut it to fit your scrapbook page and stick it in place.

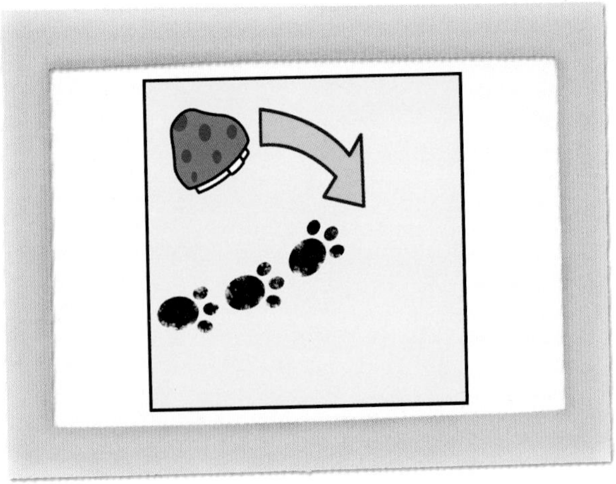

Scrapattack Tip:
Check your computer for wild-looking fonts, or ones that remind you of animals. Use them instead of handwriting on your label.

2 Dab your footprint stamp in black paint, then stamp the design across your page. Leave until the paint is dry.

3 Arrange your pressed leaves in the corners of the page. Experiment with single leaves or several leaves in a fan shape. When you're happy with the way they look, glue them in place. Leave them to dry overnight.

4 Look carefully at your photos from the trip. Can you see some great animal prints to copy? Use your coloured pencils to make your own pictures of the prints, and then cut squares to use on your page. Glue the squares onto red matting before fixing them to the page.

5 Use a small piece of brown paper for the 'At the Animal Park' journalling that forms the main title to your page. If you're not very good at drawing or designing, use vellum to trace over the heading in this book, or to trace the logo of the actual animal park you visited. Glue the heading or logo in place.

6 Choose your favourite animal photos from the trip, or use pictures that you find in magazines. Cut them out and glue them onto the leaves. Make sure you're happy with the layout of your page before you stick the pictures down.

7 Stick on your embellishments, such as your entrance ticket.

Scrapattack Tip:

If you want to make this page more personal, replace the animal prints with pictures of you and your friends at the animal park. Use animal print wrapping paper for the matting.

8 Write a phrase that works with your photos, such as 'ANIMAL MARKINGS' onto a piece of white paper. Glue the heading onto blue matting and stick it above the three animal print squares.

AT THE
ANIMAL PARK
£7
ADMITS
ONE CHILD
DATE: 9/7/05
9:37 am
ANIMAL MARKINGS

Top Dog

Make a memento of your favourite pet. This one captures the spirit of a mischievous dog! Adapt the ideas if you have a different pet animal.

You will need:
• a photo of your dog • a picture of a cat • glue • a black felt-tip pen • a newspaper • scissors

Papers:
• grey paper (light/medium/dark) • grey card • yellow paper • red paper • blue paper • white paper • green paper • ruled paper

Embellishments:
• flat wooden lolly sticks • goggle eyes

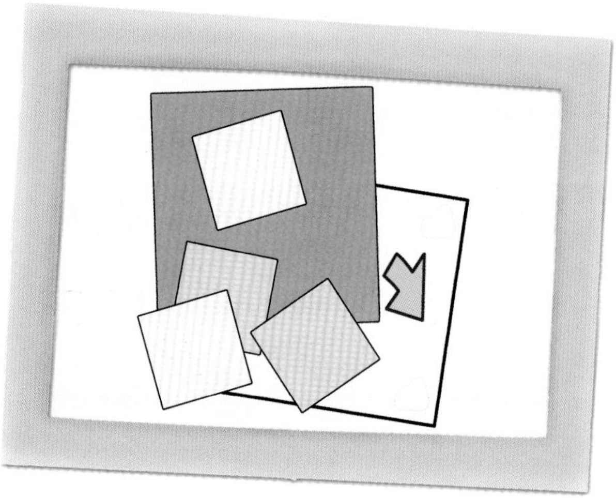

1 First make a background that looks like a pavement. Use your darkest grey paper to cover the whole of your page, then cut your other two pieces of grey paper into squares.

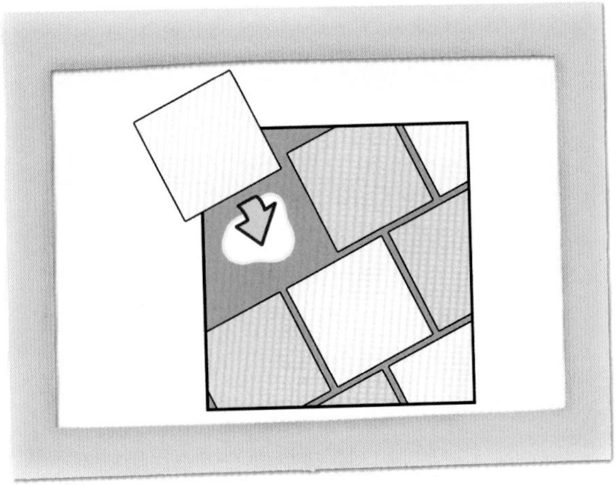

2 Glue squares of alternate colours onto the background, as shown, leaving a small gap between them. Keep a square of grey paper and put it to one side.

3 Now cut a kennel shape from your grey card. Then glue the lolly sticks lengthways onto it. Ask an adult to help you cut the sticks to size, then cut two small lengths for the the roof, and stick them on diagonally.

4 Cut a door shape from the spare square of grey paper and glue it onto the lolly sticks. Draw around the edge with a black felt-tip pen. Finally, cut around the photo of your dog and stick the head shape to the kennel. Add the goggle eyes.

5 Find an old piece of schoolwork to cut up, or scribble on your ruled paper. Cut pretend teeth marks out of the corners using scissors. Mat this onto a coloured background and arrange it carefully on your page.

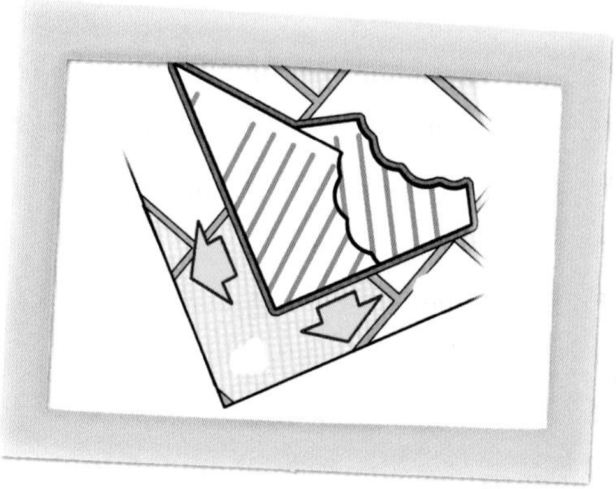

Scrapattack Tip:
Matting doesn't have to be eye-catching colours. The grey matting here is a subtle addition to the homework.

6 Cut out your picture of a cat and stick it onto card. Cut out the head and add the goggle eyes before sticking the whole thing onto your pavement background.

7 Add text explaining the page 'BAD DOG' for the chewed homework, and 'SWORN ENEMY' or 'NEXT DOOR'S CAT' if that's really what the cat is. Use letters cut from newpaper for the journalling, and add blue or green matting to the rest of the text.

Scrapattack Tip:
If you can, get an actual pawprint from your pet to stick on your page!

8 Crop your favourite picture of your dog and mat it on bright yellow paper. Add a felt-tip border if you want it to really stand out, and stick it onto the page. Then draw a pawprint onto red paper with pen, and cut it out. Finish by drawing a bone shape onto white paper. Outline the shape in pen. Add your dog's name and stick it on to your page.

BRUNO
bad dog
next door's cat
BOO BOO!

Dream Extreme

What's your favourite sport? We've designed a project around skateboarding, but you could feature any sport on this funky background.

You will need:

• a photo of you • pictures from magazines • glue • glue dots • felt-tip pens • scissors

Papers:

• green paper • cream paper • white paper • blue paper • red paper • yellow paper • wet-and-dry sandpaper (or grip tape)

Embellishments:

• plasters • cargo net

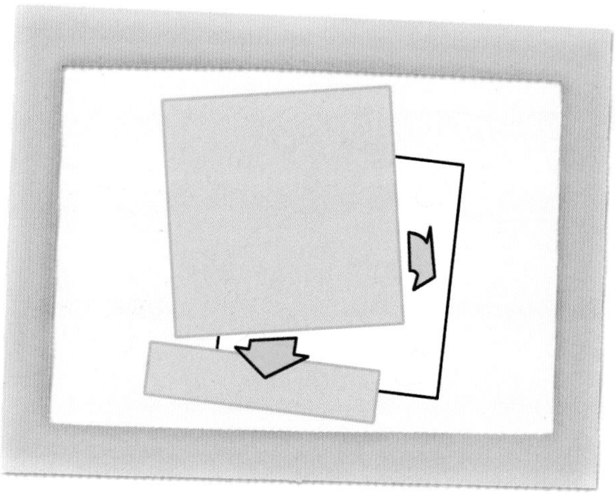

1 The first thing to make for this page is a 'camouflage' background. Use two pieces of coloured paper, one green and one cream. Cut the cream piece to fit the whole of your scrapbook page and stick it down.

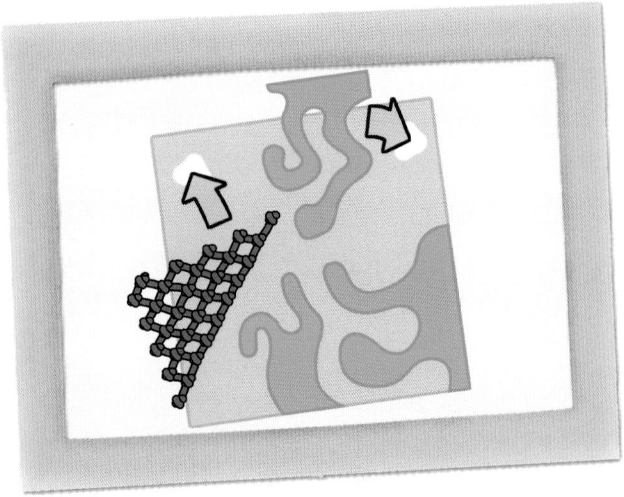

2 Now cut swirly shapes from the green piece and glue them onto the page. Then cut a piece of cargo net so that it fits into one corner, and stick it on using glue dots.

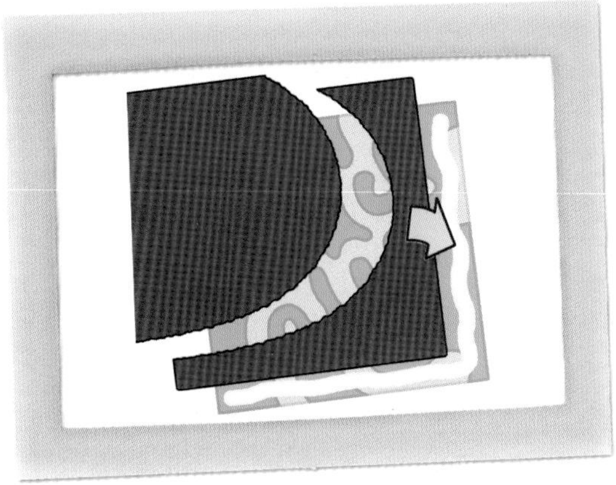

3 Cut a square of sandpaper (or grip tape) to the same size as your page. Line it up, then tear a large curve so that it fills one corner. Stick it in place, as shown.

4 Design a logo on white paper to tell everyone what your favourite sport is! Make the writing funky with bright felt-tip pens. Use the computer method (see page 17) if you're not great at lettering. Cut out your logo and stick it down.

5 Cut out your magazine pictures. Matt the main image on blue paper to make it stand out, and stick it to the centre of your page. Then cut out some smaller pictures and stick them on randomly.

Scrapattack Tip:

Use your magazines to get ideas for journalling styles. Skate magazines are full of graffiti styles that you can copy.

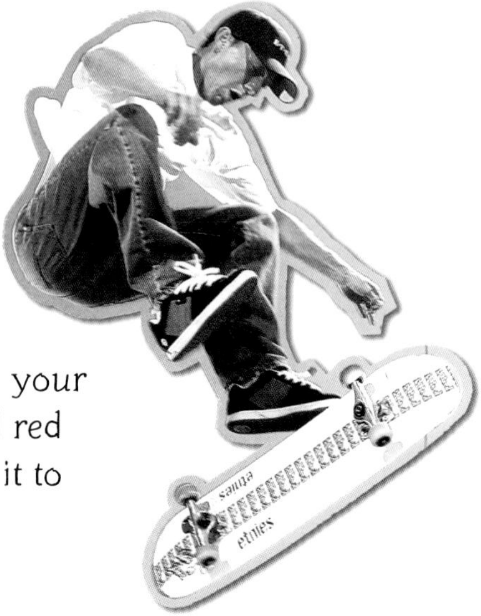

6 Now it's time to make you the star! Choose a photo of yourself in your gear, crop it and add red paper matting. Glue it to the page.

7 Use sticking plasters as a frame at the top and bottom of the photo. If you're performing a great stunt, add text such as 'OUCH' – this will make people smile!

8 Finish by drawing a logo (such as the skull and crossbones) onto yellow paper and stick it to your page.

Scrapattack Tip:
If you have lots of photos of you doing your hobby, reduce the number of magazine pictures to make room for your own images.

OUCH
SKATEBOARDING

School Daze

You will need:
• a photo of your best friend or yourself • glue
• black paint/ink • a drinking straw • scissors
• a black felt-tip pen • a white pencil

Papers:
• black paper • brown paper or card
• thick card • red paper • yellow paper
• white paper • ruled paper or old homework

Embellishments:
• an old locker key

Some people think school days are the best ever – but if you do spend yours in a daze, it's good to have something to look back on!

1 Cut a piece of black paper to cover your whole scrapbook page. Stick it in place. (If you're using brown paper for your frame, stick it onto thick card first.) Leave to dry.

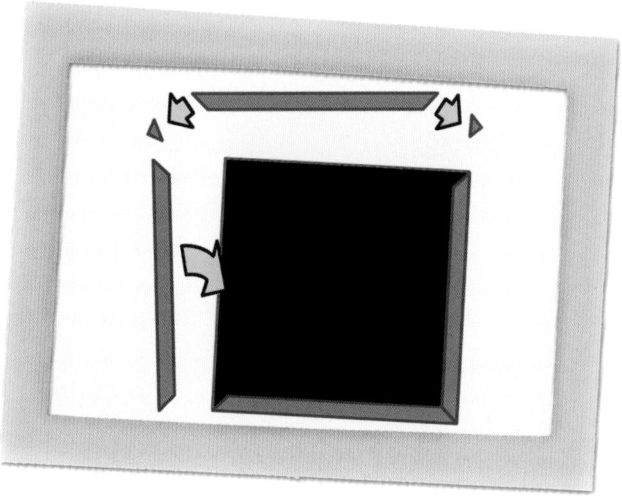

2 Cut four thin strips of brown card, long enough to frame the outside edge of your page. Fit them in place, carefully cutting each end at an angle to form the corners. (If you're feeling inspired by school, use a protractor to measure a 45° angle for each corner.) Don't glue them on just yet.

3 Find three pieces of homework that you don't need any more, or write some 'pretend homework' on the ruled paper. If you got a great mark for one of the pieces, all the better! Move them around on the page until you are happy with the layout. Trim the homework and glue it in place. Now you can stick on your brown frame.

4 Use white paper to matt your photo. If you want, draw on some funny features. Stick the matted photo on so that it overlaps the frame slightly.

…rapattack Tip:
I… …ant to spoil an actual p… …ng funny features, u… …photocopy, or scan and p… …you have a computer.

£0.40

5 To make an ink splat, pour some black ink or paint onto white paper. Use a drinking straw to blow the ink around until you get a nice 'splat' shape. Leave it to dry and then cut it out very carefully and stick it in place.

6 Now your page needs some journalling. Draw two pencil shapes, one onto red, and the other onto yellow paper. Then cut two small white paper shapes and stick them in place, as shown.

7 Add detail to the pencil shapes with a black felt-tip pen, and write 'School Days' on them. When the text is dry, glue the pencils onto your page, as shown.

8 Finish the page with some more journalling. Use white pencil to look like chalk on the blackboard, and fill the spaces on your page with doodles. Finally, stick on your locker key.

Scrapattack Tip:
As well as a locker key, you might want to add other embellishments like a school badge or logo, or a prefect's badge.

MY BEST FRIEND
HA! HA!
School
Days
WORST LESSON: SCIENCE
COOLEST TEACHER
MR BUNSEN
Insects have
do not
A+
WELL DONE!
HOMEWORK
insects have an external
is called an "exoskeleton".
to shed these
until

Top Gear

You will need:
• a photo of your dream car • a photo of yourself • two pictures of a racing driver • glue • a black felt-tip • a white pencil • scissors

Papers:
• shiny wrapping paper • white paper and card • yellow paper • tin foil • black paper • blue paper • green card

Embellishments:
• coloured cord

Fancy yourself as a racing driver with a dream car? Well, this way, you can, without even taking your driving test!

1 Cut a piece of shiny wrapping paper that fits exactly on your scrapbook page. Stick it in place. Cut two long strips of white paper and stick them to the right-hand side of the page.

2 Now make your number plate. Draw a rectangle onto yellow paper, then cut it out. Think up a cool number plate, and write the letters and numbers on the rectangle (or print them from your computer). Stick it onto your page, then outline with a black felt-tip pen.

3 Draw a circle onto black paper, and cut a smaller circle from the centre to leave a frame. Use it to frame one of your racing driver pictures (see page 29). Outline the tyre and add journalling with a white pencil. Cut tiny notches around the tyre's outside edge, then glue your photo behind the frame.

4 Glue your tyre photo to your page. Then matt a picture of your dream car onto white paper, and stick it down. Draw a downward-pointing arrow onto yellow paper, write 'MINE' on it, and stick it above your dream car.

5 Draw a key shape onto white card, and cut it out. Stick on tin foil and black paper, as shown. Draw a keyring shape onto white card, then stick blue paper on top. Make a hole in the top of your two card pieces with the end of a pencil, and join them together with cord.

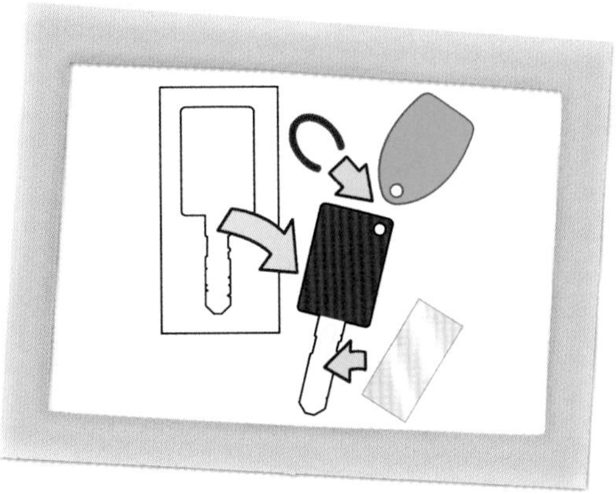

Scrapattack Tip:
Borrow a real car key to draw around to get the correct shape. Be VERY careful not to lose it!

6 Cut out your other racing driver picture and stick it onto card. Choose a photo of yourself, making sure your head is a similar size to the head of the racing driver. Cut out your head from the photo and stick it in place onto the racing driver. Now stick the whole thing onto your scrapbook page.

7 Draw a crash helmet onto green card and cut it out, following the template shown on the right. Cut out a hole for the visor to show your face. Stick on the two small pieces of yellow paper to the helmet for racing stripes.

Scrapattack Tip:
Make sure both pictures – you and the racing driver – are looking straight at the camera, or at least in the same direction as each other, so that the pictures work together.

8 Fold over the flap at the top of the helmet and use it to stick the helmet onto the top of your photo. Make sure that you can see your face through the hole. Leave the bottom part of the helmet unstuck so that you can lift it up and see the whole of your head, too.

MINE
TOP DRIVER
TOP DRIVER
DR34M C4R

Happy Birthday to Me!

You've got to have a scrapbook page for this special day – the one time of the year where everybody is concentrating just on YOU!

You will need:

• a photo of yourself • a photo of your presents • a black felt-tip pen • pipe cleaners • glue • scissors

Papers:

• wrapping paper • tissue paper • yellow paper • orange paper • white paper

Embellishments:

• ribbon • a birthday badge • a gift tag • a cake decoration

1 Use some wrapping paper kept from one of your actual presents (it doesn't matter if it is creased, see page 11). Trim your sheet to fit your scrapbook page.

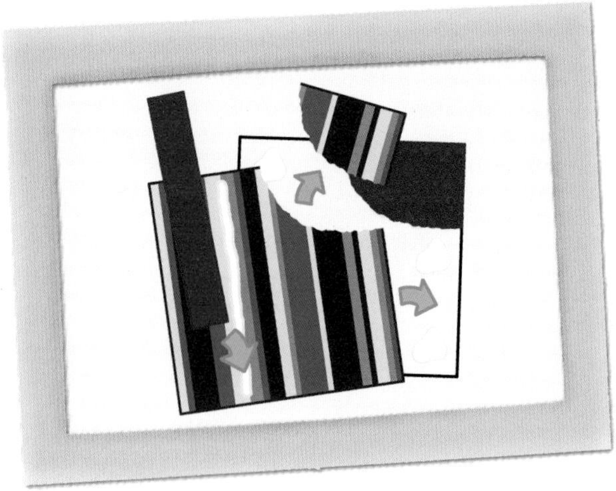

2 Stick a piece of tissue paper to the corner of your page. Now tear a corner off the wrapping paper. Stick the wrapping paper to the page, making sure there aren't any gaps where it joins the tissue paper. Stick a strip of birthday ribbon (from a gift, or your birthday cake) to the left-hand side of your page.

3 Choose a cake decoration to add to your page. If you haven't got one, you may want to make a hand-written heading for your page. See page 16 for journalling hints.

4 Stick your birthday badge in place, as shown. You will probably need to use strong glue or sticky tabs to do this.

5 Cut out two balloon shapes from your yellow and orange paper. Add white matting and stick them to the page. Stick on pieces of pipe cleaner for the strings. Crop a picture of yourself to fit on one balloon.

Scrapattack Tip:
Look for birthday die-cuts in craft shops. You may find balloon shapes and party lettering.

6 Keep one of the gift tags from your presents, and stick it to the page. Add another photograph of yourself at your party, cropped to fit inside.

7 What was your favourite birthday present? Take a photo of it, or look for a picture of it that you can cut out. Add white or coloured matting and stick it onto your page.

8 Finally, add any journalling that you need. Label the photos with 'ME!' and 'MY PRESENT', or add the date of your party. You could even make a vellum pocket (see page 22) on another page to hold your invitation replies, or photos of your friends.

Scrapattack Tip:
Try to find a gift tag with a nice message in that will remind you of your birthday.

HAPPY BIRTHDAY
MY PRESENT
ME
I'm 9

Glossary

Aged
Looking as though it has been around a long time – an effect that can be achieved with chalk.

Cropping
Cutting a photograph to change its shape or size.

Embellishments
Adding items, such as split pins, metal, wire, string and ribbon to provide interest to the page.

Focus points
The areas on the page that draw the person's eye first – can be based around a grid layout.

Framing
Putting a cardboard edge over your picture to cover the edges. Frames can also be made from items such as string, buttons or lolly sticks.

Journalling
Adding words and numbers to a page, using a variety of materials, including pens, foam letters, cut-out card pieces and stickers.

Matting
Adding extra layers behind a picture to draw attention to it. Mats are often made from paper or card, but almost any material can be used.

Memorabilia
Collected items such as leaflets and tickets that remind you of the events in the photographs,

Layout
The way in which photos, backgrounds and embellishments are arranged on a page.

Swatches
Small sample sections of patterns or colours.

Theme
The 'story' behind a page, or the common link to all the photographs eg; a football match, a holiday, or members of the same family or club.

Vellum
Semi-transparent paper, a bit like tracing paper but in different colours and patterns.